THE MEANINGS OF MODERN ART

by JOHN RUSSELL

Art Critic, The New York Times

VOLUME **5**

THE COSMOPOLITAN EYE

THE MUSEUM OF MODERN ART, NEW YORK

I. Roger de La Fresnaye
The Conquest of the Air, 1913
The Museum of Modern Art,
New York

For Roger de La Fresnaye, as for
Robert Delaunay, the world in 1913
was still a place in which all changes
were for the better—and the
invention of the aeroplane was, for
instance, something from which
nothing but good could come. (La
Fresnaye had, admittedly, a special
reason to believe this, in that his
brother was director of a firm which
manufactured aeroplanes.) The
aeroplane stood for a definitive
triumph over gravity; and that in its
turn stood—or so it then seemed—
for a new freedom from stress and
anxiety. *The Conquest of the Air* is
the complete expression of all this;
it was a great favorite of Apollinaire.

Copyright © 1975 by The Museum of Modern Art   All rights reserved   Library of Congress Catalog Card Number 72-76416
Series ISBN 0-87070-477-X   Volume 5 ISBN 0-87070-482-6   Designed by Earl Tidwell
Cover: plate I. Roger de La Fresnaye, *The Conquest of the Air,* 1913. The Museum of Modern Art, New York

Shortly before 1914 modern art began to matter, all over Europe, in ways in which it had never mattered before.

No one date, no one place, no one name can be brought forward as proof of this; but there came about a general awareness that there was such a thing as a modern sensibility, and that that sensibility had the key to modern life. People were learning to live with the fact—well put by Fernand Léger in the summer of 1913—that "the modern conception of art is the total expression of a new generation, whose condition it shares and to whose aspirations it responds."

To be modern, in this sense, was to take due note of all the changes which were being brought about in the conditions of life. It involved an acceptance of the elements of the unconscious and the irrational in human affairs. It meant overturning the tyranny of high art and high culture, and realizing that great art was just as likely to arise from close scrutiny of other areas of human activity. It meant looking at the art of other times and other peoples than those of Athens and Florence, Venice and Rome. It meant believing, with Léger again, that a billboard stuck up in the middle of a field could enrich the landscape and not desecrate it. It meant accepting the airplane and the telephone and the steel-framed building as instruments of liberation. It meant seeing our human inheritance as a whole, without fear or prejudice.

Life in those years was dipped in the dyes of the new. After 1900, when Sigmund Freud published his *Interpretation of Dreams,* the role of the unconscious was bound to come sooner or later into the forefront of art. Between 1893 and 1914 museums in Leipzig, Brussels, Cologne, Stockholm, Paris, Frankfurt, Basel and Essen installed permanent exhibitions of primitive art. In each case a whole new vocabulary was made available to young artists. In 1910 Henri Matisse was one of many attentive visitors to the great exhibition of Muslim Art in Munich. The Italian Futurist Umberto Boccioni spoke for a whole generation when he wrote in his diary in 1907 that "I want to paint the new, the fruits of our industrial age. Old walls and old palaces, old motifs and old memories nauseate me. Our feverish era makes yesterday's productions obsolete and useless." The skirl and thump of Stravinsky's *The Rite of Spring* spoke in 1913 for elemental forces too long excluded from art. Radical changes were imminent—changes as radical as those set out in the General Theory of Relativity, which Einstein had published in 1905, or in Rutherford's experiments with the atom in the years that followed.

News of these changes was carried, where art was concerned, by word of mouth, by the magazines, by one or two farsighted dealers and collectors, and by the huge conglomerate exhibitions in Paris, Berlin, London, Cologne, Munich and elsewhere, which operated before 1914 as a pacific International: a collective force which broke down national barriers, argued for a new openness of spirit, and exemplified a superabundant curiosity as to what was being done, anywhere and everywhere, in the name of the new. By 1913, when New York had a first taste of it, that pacific International had made itself felt all over Europe as the free expression of a genuinely modern sensibility.

The poet Guillaume Apollinaire (1880–1918) was, as much as anyone, the epitome of that sensibility. He had a position peculiar to himself, in that unlike most of the people who write or lecture about art he was in his own right a man of genius. In his poetry he made sense of modern life in a completely new way. Endowed with a lyrical gift of the rarest, most irresistible sort, he gave the new century the new tone for which it had been waiting; and his fragmented, unpunctuated, free-associating manner of speech became one of the basic elements in the creative practice of the 20th century. The closing section of *The Waste Land* could not have been written if T. S. Eliot had not read Apollinaire; Apollinaire stood, equally, as godfather to the best lyrics of Cole Porter and to the verbal agility which made the Beatles' song "Lucy in the Sky with Diamonds" so great a success in the late 1960s. It is well over 50 years since his two books of poems, *Alcools* and *Calligrammes,* were published; yet the poems still come across in a direct and confidential way which convinces us that Apollinaire is telling us the truth, without reserve or humbug.

In life, Apollinaire was never the high-collared Great Man. He was the involved, vulnerable, supremely human individual who got into scrapes because of the openhearted and guileless nature which made him everyone's favorite companion. When he was in love, he was unsuccessful as often as not. When society needed a scapegoat—as happened when two little statues were stolen from the Louvre—it was Apollinaire, the archetypal innocent, who was jailed on suspicion of the theft. Life made things difficult for him from the moment that he was born in Rome in 1880 of a young unmarried Polish lady and a well-connected but ne'er-do-well Italian officer, already in his middle 40s, who not long afterward disowned the relationship.

Reared first in Rome, then in Monte Carlo, and later in one or another of the towns by the Mediterranean where his mother hoped to find a protector, Apollinaire in first youth took the whole of Europe for his birthright. A natural cosmopolitan, he looked at every new place, every new book and every new person in terms of a potential adventure. If he found Nick Carter and Buffalo Bill more stimulating than Milton's *Paradise Lost,* he

1. Fernand Léger
The Wedding, 1910–11
Musée National d'Art
  Moderne, Paris

2. Fernand Léger
Woman in Blue, 1912
Öffentliche Kunstsammlung, Basel

came straight out and said so. He was spontaneity personified: "Almost all my poems have been printed as they were first written down," he wrote to a friend in 1913. He was a natural identifier, and never happier than when instinct signaled to him—in a book or a picture or a human being—a genuine life force, or a perfection not paralleled elsewhere.

All this was invaluable to him when he was introduced to Picasso in 1904. From that day onward he saw more and more of painting and painters. From 1905 until his death in 1918, he spoke up in defense of just about everyone who was going to last on the European art scene. What he said was often rather silly; but

there is no denying the record, which is that he was right in there in defense of Picasso (1905), Matisse (1907), Braque (1908), the Douanier Rousseau (1910), Robert Delaunay (1911), Kandinsky, Duchamp, Picabia, Gris and the Italian Futurists (1912), Chagall and Mondrian (1913), Larionov, Gontcharova and de Chirico (1914). Not all of them needed him; I have heard one protégé of Apollinaire say that he would write anything to fill up a page, and another that he could not tell Rubens from Rembrandt. But once again the record speaks for itself. Who introduced Picasso to Braque? Apollinaire. Who worked hardest to make Cubism acceptable to the general public? Apollinaire. Who was at the top of the visiting list for every informed foreigner who came to Paris? Apollinaire. The illustrated books on which Apollinaire

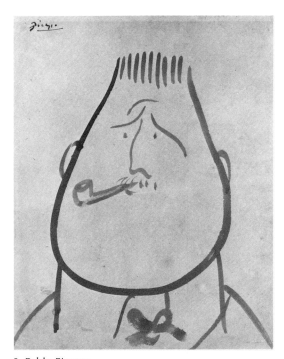

3. Pablo Picasso
Portrait of Apollinaire, 1905
Private collection, Washington, D.C.

4. Louis Marcoussis
*Portrait of Guillaume
Apollinaire,* 1912–20
The Museum of Modern
Art, New York

Louis Markus was born in Warsaw and educated there and in Cracow. He went to Paris in 1903, as a prize-winning student, and in 1910 he met Apollinaire at the circus and they became close friends. (It was at Apollinaire's suggestion that he took the name of Marcoussis, a village near Paris.) His portrait of Apollinaire, though basically Cubist in its idiom, has something of the incisive touch with the pencil which made Marcoussis a successful caricaturist.

5. (*left*) Marie Laurencin
Group of Artists, 1908
The Baltimore Museum of Art

Apollinaire was infatuated with Marie Laurencin; and through him she came to be in regular contact both with Picasso and with Fernande Olivier, who was Picasso's mistress at the time. In this painting Apollinaire, Picasso and the two ladies would seem to be getting on very well; but Fernande Olivier never took to Marie Laurencin, and in her memoirs she wrote—among much else of a disparaging sort—that Marie Laurencin "had the face of a goat, with eyelids drawn back and myopic eyes set too close to a pointed, inquisitive nose which was always rather red at the tip."

6. Albert Gleizes
Harvest Threshing, 1912
The Solomon R. Guggenheim Museum, New York

worked with Derain in 1909 and with Dufy in 1911 are classics of their kind. Apollinaire gave Orphism its name in 1913. From February, 1912, onward he edited *Les Soirées de Paris,* as brilliant a review of art and literature as has ever existed. When he and Delaunay went to Germany in 1913 he made an unforgettable impression on the young Max Ernst. In 1917 he invented the word "Surrealism." When he got married in 1918 Picasso was a witness at the ceremony; and nothing in Picasso's work bespeaks a more heartfelt affection than the long series of portrait drawings of Apollinaire—Apollinaire plain, Apollinaire fantasized, Apollinaire in health and strength, and Apollinaire with the head wound he sustained as a willing soldier in 1916. Apollinaire was not always right about art—who ever was?—but one of the greatest periods of European art bears the mark of his passage over and over again.

He did more for art, and for artists, than just write about them. The conditions of his life had made him the most adroit of persuaders—who else has had a plaque put up in his honor on the wall of a hotel which he left without paying the bill?—and he never begrudged time spent on behalf of the new. When the minor or auxiliary Cubists (among them Gleizes, Metzinger, Delaunay, Léger and Le Fauconnier) determined to show together at the Salon des Indépendants in April, 1911, it was Apollinaire who acted as their champion; when they were invited to Brussels,

again as a group, two months later, it was Apollinaire who prefaced the catalogue. What he said was not all true, but it did very clearly indicate what Gleizes, for one, was aiming to do. He was getting ready, Apollinaire said, to tackle "the vast subjects which yesterday's painters in their timidity had never dared to wrest from the presumptuous, outdated and tedious daubers of the official Salons." Today we know that "vast subjects" played no part in Cubist painting as it was brought to perfection by Picasso, Braque and Gris. Their subject matter was limited, concise, and most often emotionally neutral. Apollinaire unwittingly let slip the fact that Gleizes and Metzinger had no idea of what Cubism was really about and were using it simply as a way of giving a look of modernity to undertakings which fundamentally were pedestrian and conventional. Once we have read his preface we see at once why Gleizes' enormous *Harvest Threshing* (fig. 6) had ended up looking like a Salon picture with the fidgets.

THE DOUANIER BREAKS THE GROUND

Sometimes Apollinaire was oddly slow off the mark. Henri Rousseau was, for instance, so fundamental to the evolution of a modern sensibility that Apollinaire might have been expected to get the point of him at once. (Rousseau's nickname, "le Douanier," was a friendly exaggeration, insofar as he was not a customs officer, as might be supposed, but simply a minor official—from 1871 to 1885—in the Paris municipal toll service.) A great part of European Surrealism is foreshadowed in Rousseau's unhurrying, matter-of-fact notation of the most startling and incongruous of images. There was nothing merely quaint or folksy, moreover, about Rousseau's handling of landscape; Picasso profited by its fearless conceptual approach in the paintings which he made in the autumn of 1908, and by 1909 it was common ground with many serious artists that Rousseau personified that clear break with conventional, "educated" painting which was an important element in the modern sensibility.

Apollinaire wrote in 1908 that Rousseau "does not know either what he wants nor where he is going. . . . He should have stayed an artisan." However, in 1909 he came to know Rousseau well, and sat for him for his portrait. From his friend Delaunay, and doubtless from Picasso too, he learned that Rousseau was a key figure in living art. When Rousseau showed *The Dream* in 1910 (pl. II), Apollinaire seized the chance not only to make amends on his own account but to emphasize that Rousseau had just about every good artist in Paris behind him. Here is his classic account of *The Dream:* "On an 1830-style sofa, a naked woman is asleep. All around her is a tropical forest swarming with monkeys and birds of paradise. A lion and a lioness pass calmly by,

II. Henri Rousseau
The Dream, 1910
The Museum of Modern Art, New York

7. Paul Gauguin
Loss of Virginity, 1890–91
Chrysler Museum at Norfolk, Virginia

The first year of the new century produced one of the most influential books of modern times: Sigmund Freud's *The Interpretation of Dreams* (1900). Already in the 1890s art had tackled the secret life of the unconscious. Gauguin for one, and Rousseau for another, had shown how sleep brings us face to face with fears and temptations and repressed wishes which we prefer not to acknowledge in our waking lives. In Gauguin's *Loss of Virginity* the young girl is innocence personified, in waking terms, and a sacred circle of fire is there to protect her; but that does not prevent the fox, symbol of insidious sexuality, from laying his paw on her breast while she is sleeping. (Nor does it prevent her from giving him the most trustful of welcomes.) In Rousseau's *The Sleeping Gypsy* the conventional patterns of savagery, fear and danger are suspended; the dream takes precedence over the conditions of everyday and a strange immunity envelops the sleeping woman.

8. Henri Rousseau
The Sleeping Gypsy, 1897
The Museum of Modern Art,
New York

9. Franz Marc
*Half-length Portrait of
Henri Rousseau with
Long Mustache,* 1911
Städtische Galerie im
Lenbachhaus, Munich

At the time of his death in 1910 Henri Rousseau was beloved of his fellow-painters all over Europe. Franz Marc adapted the traditional techniques of Bavarian glass-painting for this little memorial portrait, which puts the Douanier where he belongs—among the patron-saints of modern art.

10. Henri Rousseau
The Poet and His Muse,
1909
Kunstmuseum, Basel

In 1909 the Douanier Rousseau painted this subject twice over and with great affection, though the portrait of Marie Laurencin was none too flattering.

while a mysterious Negro plays on his pipe. No one can deny that this is a very beautiful painting. . . . This year nobody, I think, will dare to laugh at Rousseau. . . . Ask the painters. They are unanimous in their admiration. They admire everything in *The Dream,* let me tell you—yes, even the Louis-Philippe sofa lost in the primeval forest—and they are right."

"I, too, am a painter" was one of Apollinaire's working titles for his *Calligrammes;* and although it was not true in any literal sense, there was nothing that he liked better than to identify with his friends' intentions. Not all of them encouraged this—it is very unlikely that either Picasso or Braque confided in Apollinaire during the great years of Cubism—but Apollinaire found that Delaunay, for one, was delighted to do so. He was close to the Delaunays—he moved in with them for two months in the fall of 1912, at a time of intense private distress for himself, and he spent the summer of 1913 with them in a house party which also included Marc Chagall, the poet Blaise Cendrars, and the American painter Patrick Henry Bruce—and it must have been of Delaunay that he was thinking when he wrote in the winter of 1911–12 that "the secret ambition of the advanced young painters is to create a form of pure painting. This completely new kind of plastic expression is still in its infancy and is not yet as abstract as it aspires to be."

The new painting had nothing to do with the Cubism of Picasso, Braque and Gris, which was fundamentally a down-to-earth activity; but it did make sense in the context of the evolution of Delaunay, with which Apollinaire was intimately familiar. Delaunay in 1909 had been deeply influenced by Cézanne, but like his friend Léger he wanted to get more of the throb and bluster of modern life into his work than Cézanne had ever aimed for. In fact he was altogether too boisterous, in 1910–11, to keep in line with the principles of pure Cubism: "But they're painting with *cobwebs,* these people!" was his first reaction when he saw Cubist paintings by Picasso and Braque which were virtually monochromatic. He liked strong contrasts of color and spectacular dislocations of form; and—above all in the Eiffel Tower series (fig. 14)—he liked subject matter which had already an epic resonance.

9

III. Sonia Delaunay
The Bal Bullier, 1913
Musée National d'Art Moderne, Paris

By his marriage in 1910 to the Russian-born painter Sonia Terk, Robert Delaunay acquired a partner whose gifts were no less powerful than his own, and whose contribution to many departments of Parisian life were unmistakable for their wit, their zest, and their sense of style. *The Bal Bullier* bears the name of what was for many years the liveliest of the Parisian dance-halls; in the scale of its ambition and in the energy and determination with which it was carried through, it can stand with the most monumental of modern paintings. Sonia

Delaunay had learned from Gauguin and from Robert Delaunay how to make flat patches of color sing out in harmony; but in the observation of the individual dancers (enlaced, many of them, in the complications of that sinuous novelty, the tango) she displayed a feminine high spirit that was all her own; and in her ability to maintain the liveliest of movement across a broad narrow area she anticipated the panoramic and all-enveloping effects of Cinemascope.

11. Robert Delaunay
The Cardiff Team, 1912–13
Stedelijk van Abbe Museum, Eindhoven

12. Robert Delaunay
Sun Disks, 1912–13
The Museum of Modern Art, New York

13. Robert Delaunay
Sun, Tower and Airplane, 1913
Albright-Knox Art Gallery, Buffalo, N.Y.

Like many artists who fall just short of greatness, Delaunay was not at all shy of making big claims for himself later in life. "We, the first Cubists" was one phrase in his notebooks, and he also felt that he had a great impact on Expressionism, on films like *The Cabinet of Dr. Caligari* (1919), and on postrevolutionary Russian theater. But where he did undeniably exert an influence was with the series of paintings which was made during the period of his closest friendship with Apollinaire. These were what Apollinaire called his Orphic paintings, and they were begun at Louveciennes, on the outskirts of Paris, in the first half of 1913. Delaunay had always hoped to effect the free interaction of color, and he felt that the Cubist system of interlocking planes was as injurious to this free interaction as was the niggly microscopic structuring of pointillist painting. He wanted to banish Cubist faceting, and he also wanted to banish the gradations of color which had previously facilitated a smooth transition from one color area to another. Finally he decided that color was best handled in the form of round, unmodulated discs of pure color, initially prompted by celestial bodies but now freed from all figurative intention.

Delaunay's work had had since 1909 a direct emotional vibration which was independent of any systematic intellectual structuring and made it particularly attractive to painters in other countries. Perhaps some of them sensed — especially in Germany — that of all the French painters he was the most likely to lift off into the kind of pure painting, unballasted by any figurative concerns, which seemed likely on philosophico-mystical grounds to turn up sooner or later. Certainly Delaunay was courted from 1911 onward by the small Russo-German group of painters in Munich who had just decided to band together under the name of Der Blaue Reiter (The Blue Rider).

KANDINSKY HEADS A GENERAL MOVE TO MUNICH

Munich before 1914 was a stronghold of the pacific International. It had always been a city open to great ideas and eager, often in a deadpan, literal way, to annex them. Visitors found echoes of Athens and Florence in its architecture and of English landscape gardening in the huge park which came right into the middle of the city. There was a tradition of the new in Munich, also. Wagner had been performed there when theaters elsewhere were closed to him. In 1893, the year in which Thomas Mann settled in Munich, a new exhibiting society called the Munich Secession brought together Franz von Stuck, Arnold Böcklin, Lovis Corinth, Max Liebermann, Max Slevogt and others who were then regarded as advanced artists. In 1895–96 three impor-

14. Robert Delaunay
Eiffel Tower, 1910
The Solomon R. Guggenheim
Museum, New York

15. Cover design for
Jugend, August 14, 1897,
by H. Christiansen
Published: Munich and
Leipzig, G. Hirth

Developments in fine art soon spilled over into the magazines. Here, for instance, on the cover of a Munich weekly, *Jugend*, is an image that might have been lifted, unchanged, from Symbolist painting.

IV. Wassily Kandinsky
Landscape near Murnau, 1909
The Solomon R. Guggenheim Museum, New York

14

V. Wassily Kandinsky
Composition No. 2, 1910
The Solomon R. Guggenheim Museum, New York

tant magazines were founded there: *Pan, Jugend* (fig. 15) and *Simplicissimus.* Art Nouveau produced one of its most celebrated triumphs in the façade which August Endell designed for a Munich photographer's studio in 1898. Good acting has always been treasured in Munich, and in 1901 the new Schauspielhaus set a new standard for theater architecture.

All this attracted foreigners; and the Munich art world was remarkable above all for its large Russian contingent. This was made up for the most part not of beginners but of mature men and women who had had experience of other cities and had finally fixed on Munich as the most stimulating place in which to live. The leader of this large group was Wassily Kandinsky, who had arrived in Munich in 1897 at the age of thirty. He had not always meant to be an artist; only a few months before he arrived in Munich he had been offered a professorship in law at a Russian university, and whereas his fellow Russians in Munich had mostly been art students in Moscow or St. Petersburg, Kandinsky had followed a wide range of interdisciplinary interests before settling for painting as his main activity. He was, for instance, something of an amateur ethnographer, and he had traveled in parts of Russia in which a timeless folk-world was still intact. In those remote provinces, color was everywhere: houses were painted inside and out with a richness, a power of invention, and a spiritual energy which were deeply impressive to Kandinsky. He felt while there as if he were living in a world that was all art; and when he became an artist himself his ambition was not to produce beautiful and lucrative objects but to communicate something that was of vital importance to the spiritual well-being of mankind.

Kandinsky's maternal grandmother had come from the Baltic provinces of Russia, where the traditional culture was markedly Germanic, and from her he had learned not only the German language but the elaborate mythic structures of German folklore. This predisposed him to feel at home in Munich, which had the further advantage of having, in those days, a great deal of the emblematic color—canary-yellow mailboxes, bright blue streetcars, apricot-yellow baroque façades and burnished gold cupolas—which Kandinsky had prized in Moscow. Fixed, recurrent color was a necessity of life to him; from his childhood in Moscow he needed to be assured that at a certain time, every day, certain colors would be on hand. He found all this in Munich; and from Bavaria in general he got a parallel reassurance: the knowledge that certain ancient crafts—painting on glass, above all—were still being carried on with undiminished poetry. Munich was absolutely right for Kandinsky, and he lost no time in making an impression there.

16

16. Wassily Kandinsky
Phalanx: First Exhibition, 1901
The Museum of Modern Art, New York

17. Wassily Kandinsky
*Russian Beauty in a
Landscape,* 1905
Städtische Galerie im
Lenbachhaus,
Munich

He had, among other things, a very good sense of timing. He knew when situations were ripe for himself, and he knew when they were ripe for others. He knew when to start a liberal art school in Munich called the "Phalanx" (fig. 16), just after the turn of the century, and he knew when to close it up (in 1902) and go on his travels. He knew when to start an association of artists in Munich (the Neue Künstlervereinigung, in 1909), and he knew when to secede from it (two years later) and found The Blue Rider. He was ideally open-minded—in its second exhibition, in the winter of 1910–11, the Neue Künstlervereinigung gave Picasso, Braque, Derain, Rouault, Vlaminck and van Dongen the freedom of its walls—and when The Blue Rider came to publish its *Almanac,* in December, 1912, the table of contents read like an index to modern sensibility. Everything was there: the perfected internationalism, the cross-references to theater and music, the sharp focus on primitive art, the total rejection of cultural hierarchies, the belief that much could be learned from children's art, and from peasant crafts, and indeed from anything at all that was done without thought of academic sanction.

Kandinsky was alive to all this, but he was also alive to his own particular needs. Even the name of The Blue Rider corresponded to them; he said later that "Franz Marc loved horses, and I loved riders, and we both loved blue. It was as simple as that." Kandinsky wrote later in his fragmentary memoirs, "The horse carries the rider with strength and speed, but it is the rider who guides the horse. Talent can bring an artist to great heights, again with strength and speed, but it is for the artist to direct his talent."

19. Alexej von Jawlensky
Landscape, Murnau, 1910
Kunstmuseum, Düsseldorf

Jawlensky had been for 19 years a professional soldier in the Russian army before he finally got out and met Kandinsky in 1897. His inclinations had always lain in the direction of art; and from 1905 onward he was acquainted with Matisse. He was one of the earliest and most substantial adherents of Kandinsky's Neue Künstlervereinigung (New Association of Artists) in Munich, and when he came to paint the familiar landscape of Murnau in 1910 he piled slab upon slab of pure cobalt in the sky and gave a particular sharp yellow to the church tower as it soared above the little town.

20. Wassily Kandinsky
Panel (3), 1914
The Museum of Modern Art, New York

21. Wassily Kandinsky
Panel (4), 1914
The Museum of Modern Art, New York

Timing was vital: "There comes a predestined hour," he wrote in The Blue Rider *Almanac,* "when the time is ripe for decisions." What Kandinsky was waiting for in the first years of this century was the moment at which new values could be promulgated and mankind set on the path toward redemption.

It was in the course of this, and not as an aesthetic exercise, that Kandinsky came to paint abstract pictures. Such is our historical conditioning that for years it was very difficult to think of abstract painting as dictated rather by inner necessity than by one episode or another in a holy war between abstraction and figuration. Abstract painting was something that people had to be for or against, as they were for or against corporal punishment or universal free trade. To have "painted the first abstract picture" became a brevet of honor, like being the first man to step on to the moon. Even Kandinsky in later years staked out his claim, for fear that someone would boast of having beaten him to it.

But the truth is that there was nothing willed or doctrinaire about Kandinsky's abstract paintings. Nor was there a Monday on which he was painting representational pictures and a Tuesday on which he gave them up forever. His development is vastly more complicated than that, and not the least of its complications is the fact that Kandinsky actually desiderated an element of mystery in the whole matter. In the winter of 1911–12 he defined the content of his art as "the communication of what is secret by what is secret"; and it is on his terms, and not on those of the internal polemics of art, that we should look at the pictures.

It is relevant, for instance, that by 1909 Kandinsky had seen enough of Fauve painting to know what was likely to happen when, in his own words, he "let himself go" before nature. "Not worrying about houses or trees," he wrote, "I spread strips and dots of paint on the canvas with my palette knife and let them sing out as loudly as I could." French painting had given the green light for this in the fall of 1905; Kandinsky had been in Paris for much of the following year. But we must also consider what can be called the Central European element. The need to identify with strong, unbroken color was fundamental to the new, unshackled spiritual life as it was imagined by poets and novelists and painters alike. Looking at Kandinsky's *Landscape near Murnau* of 1909 (pl. IV), where clouds and blossom are almost interchangeable and the rearing irregular forms careen this way and that, we might well remember the painter-hero of Hermann Hesse's long story *Klingsor's Last Summer.* That story was written in 1919–20 as an elegy for the lost hopes and betrayed ambitions of the world before 1914; and there is something of Kandinsky in the paintings which Hesse sets before us—"those free paraphrases on the world of phenomena, those strange,

22. Wassily Kandinsky
Study for "Landscape with a Tower," 1908
The Solomon R. Guggenheim Museum, New York

23. Wassily Kandinsky
Pastorale, No. 132, 1911
The Solomon R. Guggenheim Museum, New York

19

VI. Wassily Kandinsky
Mountain, 1909
Städtische Galerie im
Lenbachhaus,
Munich

glowing, and yet dreamily tranquil pictures with their twisted trees and plantlike houses." Hesse goes on, "At the time his palette had been reduced to a few extremely vivid colors—cadmium yellow and red, Veronese green, emerald, cobalt, cobalt violet, French vermilion and crimson lake."

Beyond this, there is the fact that the subject matter of Kandinsky's Murnau landscapes meant more to him, in a concrete symbolical way, than the little French fishing village of Collioure meant to Matisse or L'Estaque to Derain. For Kandinsky, the church, the mountain, the still waters of the Staffelsee, and the horse and its rider were the forerunners of a vision of the Apocalypse; and when that vision finally presented itself the church, the mountain, the lake and the rider were all still there. Agents of the Apocalypse, they signaled the extent to which everyday vision had been overthrown and revelation had taken its place. Subject matter might be "a hindrance," as Kandinsky said later; but it was a necessary hindrance, in that without it the observer might lapse into mere passive aesthetic enjoyment. The purpose of art was to prepare the observer for the new realm of the spirit which was about to begin; only if enough people became aware of its possibilities would Madame Blavatsky's prophecy be fulfilled and the earth become, in the 21st century, "a heaven by comparison with what it is now."

Madame Blavatsky (1831–1891) spoke for occultist and theosophical beliefs which to most people, now as then, seem windy and unfounded. But in the pacific International there were many intelligent people who took her, and her fellow-theosophist Rudolf Steiner, quite seriously. Kandinsky, for one, saluted Madame Blavatsky for having been the first person (as he saw it) to see that what were then called "savages" could have valuable lessons for the European. And he seems to have believed, with Steiner, that the Revelation of St. John foreshadowed an era in which great catastrophes, then already imminent, would be followed by the attainment of an undreamed-of spirituality and the rebirth of mankind. Kandinsky saw it as his duty to make this known through his paintings: not in an obvious, literal, echo-less way, but not in a totally enigmatic way either. The vibration had to get through to those who were ready to receive it.

That is the background to the paintings of 1909–14 which have too often been looked at primarily in the context of whether or not they can be called "abstract." Kandinsky in these paintings was concerned to give something away, but not too much, of his secret intentions. His pyramidal *Mountain,* 1909 (pl. VI), should for instance be read in terms of Rudolf Steiner's belief that the fulfilled artist, "immersed in the hidden, internal treasures of his art," was "a fellow-worker much to be envied for his part in

24. Wassily Kandinsky
Improvisation No. 30, 1913
The Art Institute of Chicago

building the spiritual pyramid which will reach to heaven." Steiner lived in Munich, and Kandinsky very probably had personal contact with him. He is said to have heard him lecture on Goethe's *Faust;* several of his friends and colleagues were wholehearted Steinerians; Kandinsky's theatrical experiments run close to Steiner's. Kandinsky's work from 1909 to 1914 can best be read, in short, as a personal commentary, idiosyncratic but nonetheless perfectly coherent, on Steiner's convictions. Kandinsky was by nature a mystic; not only did Steiner give him subject matter that called for the scale of epic, but he suggested a parallel between that subject matter and the creative process as Kandinsky had come to understand it. Making art, Kandinsky had decided, was like making the world in miniature: "painting is like a violent and thunder-wracked collision between different worlds that are destined to create a new world by fighting one another. . . . Every work of art comes into being in the way that the universe came into being—as a result of catastrophes in which all the instruments play out of tune until finally there sings out what

25. Wassily Kandinsky
Winter Study with Church, 1911
The Solomon R Guggenheim Museum,
New York

we call 'the music of the spheres.'" What he painted under the impulse of these beliefs were not so much "abstract paintings" as images whose implications were coded to a greater or a lesser degree.

These images did, however, spring in part from ideas which predated Kandinsky's acquaintance with Steiner. Ever since his childhood in Moscow he had believed that colors had an autonomous life of their own. In his book *On the Spiritual in Art,* written in 1910, he said, for instance, that a strong yellow stood for aggression, that orange rang out like a church bell, and that green stood for smugness and passivity. Ever since he had seen one of Monet's *Haystacks* in Russia and had not at first been able to decipher it, he had believed that a painting can have an impact on the observer which is quite independent of its subject matter. To that extent he thought of an abstract, nonreferential art as the ideal art of the future. But he also foresaw that it could easily

lapse into something of merely decorative interest, "like a necktie or a carpet"; for this reason he continued to secrete coded messages within what might have been taken for abstract paintings. From the fall of 1911 these paintings were much talked about in his circle, and Paul Klee, for one, wrote in his diary that "they appear to have no subject. Very strange paintings, they are." But even more relevant to this context is the little painting which was produced in 1913 by a much closer associate of Kandinsky's, August Macke. *Making Fun of The Blue Rider* (fig. 26) is its title, and it allies a characteristic Kandinskian scene of upheaval to a group of satirical portraits of Blue Rider adherents; the code was cracked this time by someone who was well placed to know what it was.

The Blue Rider was not an association of equals, like the Impressionists, but a dictatorship in which Kandinsky and Franz Marc showed whatever seemed to them to be right, without

22

26. August Macke
Making Fun of The Blue Rider, 1913
Städtische Galerie im Lenbachhaus, Munich

The activities of The Blue Rider were in general unremittingly earnest. But that they had a lighter side is clear from this sketch by August Macke, which includes recognizable portraits of Kandinsky, Marc, Gabriele Münter, August and Marie Macke and Herwarth Walden, editor of the magazine *Der Sturm* and director of the gallery which was associated with it.

27. Franz Marc
The Unfortunate Land of Tyrol, 1913
The Solomon R. Guggenheim Museum, New York

"He lived on an alp," someone once said of Franz Marc, "with sheep and cows and a couple of good books." And for several years Marc made a paradise on earth from these simple elements. But in 1913 that paradise began to spoil. Whether from a premonition of World War I, or from an intimation of some even more definitive downward turn in human affairs, Marc began to paint pictures which were haunted by loss and alienation. *The Unfortunate Land of Tyrol* prefigures a scene of desolation such as was to be found on every European battlefront between 1914 and 1918. Its broken, jagged and inconclusive formal structure is the complete antithesis of all that Marc had previously stood for: positive color, unlimited energy, formal rhythms strongly carried through, and a sense of limitless well-being in the presence of the animal world.

bothering about anyone else's opinions or wishes. Marc was a man of considerable intellectual powers; he had a wide-ranging curiosity, and although he did not share Kandinsky's theosophical beliefs he was convinced that his generation stood at a hingepoint in the history of the world. In paintings like *The Blue Horse,* 1911 (pl. VII), he used color in a free and arbitrary manner, so that familiar images would vanish from view (like a water hen, as he himself put it) only to surface in a new guise and a new place. Later, and as a premonition of the war in which he would shortly be killed, he painted the animal kingdom in a state of decay and dissolution (as in *The Unfortunate Land of Tyrol*; fig. 27). "It is logical," he wrote, "to paint such pictures before a war, as a constructive act which makes the future visible."

Kandinsky, in all this, moved with the ordered assurance of one who was not so much "an artist" in the precarious or bohemian sense as a member of the professional classes who had turned to art and was doing uncommonly well at it. There is no reason to disbelieve what he wrote in his memoirs—that before perfecting a new idea he was in a state of extreme inner tension, and that the sense of inner necessity which was fundamental to all such advances had to be stalked through days filled with restless anxiety and nights haunted by "fantastic dreams full of terror and delight." But none of this showed in his public persona, which could have been that of a military man (two of his Russian colleagues in Munich were retired army officers) or a doctor in a very good way of business. In particular, he was completely at ease with his Russian inheritance. That inheritance was all gain, as far as he was concerned; and he certainly had no reason to feel that conditions in Russia had been hostile to his personal development.

23

VII. Franz Marc
The Blue Horse I, 1911
Städtische Galerie im Lenbachhaus, Munich

"How does a horse see the world?" Franz Marc wrote in one of his letters. "It is a wretched, soulless convention which causes us to paint animals in a landscape which corresponds to our own vision. We should rather try to sink ourselves in the soul of the animal portrayed, so that in time we see the landscape as he sees it. . . ." Blue was the color of hope, for Franz Marc, and *The Blue Horse* radiates a sturdy optimism, with the whole of Nature responding to the horse as he stands squarely on all his four feet.

THE FRANCO-RUSSIAN ALLIANCE

In this, he was in striking contrast to Marc Chagall, who arrived in Paris from Russia in 1910 and in time became a friend of both Apollinaire and Delaunay. The pacific International was very much in operation at this time in Franco-Russian artistic relations; by 1914 a young painter in Moscow, in particular, had easy access to the great paintings by Matisse and Picasso which two Russian collectors, Shchukin and Morosov, had brought together, and there had been loan shows of recent French painting which have never been surpassed for quality and discernment. For the well-bred, well-fed, much-traveled and personally not seldom irresistible aesthetes who made up the art world of Moscow and St. Petersburg, life had just about every advantage. It was very pleasant before 1914 to go to Paris as the countryman of Diaghilev, who had given Western Europe a new idea of what the ballet could be, and of Chaliapin, who was acclaimed as the greatest singer-actor in history, and of Scriabin, who had given a new dimension to concert life. (Scriabin's tone-poem *Prometheus* was the subject of a close and eulogious analysis in The Blue Rider *Almanac*.)

Among the Russians who visited Paris at that time were Mikhail Larionov and Nathalie Gontcharova, who between them were about to set Russian painting on a new path. Just how they did it we shall see later; the point here is that they would have found it much harder to do without the enlightened patronage of Diaghilev, who sent them to Paris in 1906—and, in a more general way, without the atmosphere of informed curiosity which the pacific International had created in Moscow. That curiosity was ubiquitous at that time, and when Larionov and Gontcharova came to live in Paris in 1914 Apollinaire wrote about them in *Les Soirées de Paris* as established and substantial figures, co-partners in the creation of "a universal art in which painting, sculpture, poetry, music and even science in all its manifold aspects will be combined." To be a gifted young artist in such conditions was to be one of a privileged brotherhood for whom national frontiers had no meaning.

Things did not however look quite so well if, like Chagall, you were Jewish, came from what was comparatively speaking a town in the sticks, and could not even get permission to live in St. Petersburg, much less to study there, unless you were registered as a domestic servant. Chagall survived all this, but he survived by using his art as a charm against alienation. In other words, he kept sane by painting an alternative world. It was in some respects a world of the most patient and faithful realism; a painting like *Birth* (fig. 29) is "true to life" in a way that strikes us at once

28. Nathalie Gontcharova
"Le Coq d'Or"
(Scenery design for Diaghilev's Ballets Russes, Paris, 1914)
The Museum of Modern Art, New York

Rimsky-Korsakov was a master of spangled and glittering orchestral timbres; and in her designs for his opera *Le Coq d'Or* Nathalie Gontcharova found a precise visual equivalent for the intoxicating sounds which carried all before them when they were heard for the first time in western Europe. It was to be quite sure of this kind of authenticity that Diaghilev had invited Larionov and Gontcharova to Paris.

29. Marc Chagall
Birth, 1911
The Art Institute of Chicago

30. Marc Chagall
Self-Portrait with Seven Fingers, 1912
Stedelijk Museum,
Amsterdam

32. Marc Chagall
Half Past Three (The Poet),
1911
Philadelphia Museum
of Art

31. Marc Chagall
Burning House, 1913
The Solomon R. Guggenheim Museum, New York

33. Marc Chagall
Homage to Apollinaire,
1911–12
Stedelijk van Abbe
Museum, Eindhoven

The subject matter of Chagall's *Homage to Apollinaire* is a condensed version of the story of Adam and Eve. In a single image we see Eve, sprung from Adam's rib but still a part of him, in the act of offering Adam the apple of knowledge which will cause them to be expelled from Paradise.

The pierced heart which stands for friendship is surrounded by the names of four close friends: Apollinaire, the poet Blaise Cendrars, Herwarth Walden, and Ricciotto Canudo, friend of the Futurist leader F. T. Marinetti and editor of the avant-garde review *Montjoie*.

34. Marc Chagall
Over Vitebsk (after a painting
of 1914), 1915–20
The Museum of Modern Art,
New York

as authentic, and the wooden house in *Burning House* (fig. 31) could not sit more squarely on the canvas. Chagall in first youth had a way of hugging fact—of holding it ever more closely to him—as if by hugging it tight enough he could remake the world. He was a wonderful storyteller—later he became one of the great book illustrators—but his first purpose was to heal the hurt of living in a society which denied him certain fundamental human rights.

He did this in two ways. First, he used color to say to the observer, "This is not the world as you know it." Second, he used fantasy to show that at a given moment the events portrayed on the canvas became a revision of the known life and an emblem of a better one. The Jew in life, in the little town of Vitebsk, was a tethered man. He had none of the mobility, social and geographical, which was the birthright of the European Gentile before 1914. He was not precisely a captive, but he was not a free man

either. Chagall dealt with this by positing an alternative world in which the Jew had supernatural powers. He could soar above the rooftops like a Montgolfier balloon, he could cross the town in one easy stride, he could make life dance to the tunes which he drew from his green violin, and when he met the girl of his dreams he could put the whole of Vitebsk to sleep as he and she whirled around and above it as its unchallenged prince and princess. Imagination was the outcast's revenge in Vitebsk; and the paintings came from an inner necessity as strong as Kandinsky's and a good deal more immediate in its action. Later—much later—Chagall fell back on winsome replication; but in the first years his was a healing art, and the interaction of personalities between him and Apollinaire was predictably vivid. (Chagall's *Homage to Apollinaire*, fig. 33, is one of the most successful of his early Parisian paintings; and Apollinaire in *Calligrammes* dedicated a poem called "A travers l'Europe" to Chagall.)

VIII. Mikhail Larionov
Soldier on a Horse, c. 1908–11
The Tate Gallery, London

At a crucial stage in his career Mikhail Larionov had to spend nine months
(1908–09) in the Russian army. From this he derived a wealth of new subject
matter which was ideally suited to what he wanted to achieve: the mingling of
Russian folk art with sophisticated European attitudes to color and form.

IX. Marc Chagall
Calvary, 1912
The Museum of Modern Art, New York

Chagall impressed his friends in Paris by the immediacy, and the sense of total involvement, with which he recreated the facts of his childhood and first youth in Russia. Those memories were not "recollected in tranquillity"; they were relived. And when Chagall turned (as here) to a New Testament subject he still worked with the materials that lay nearest to hand: his own experience of suffering in a particular place at a particular time. In October, 1913, Blaise Cendrars, poet and globe-trotter, wrote of Chagall that "because he had spent his whole childhood on the Cross and was astonished that he was still alive," it was as natural for him to paint the figure of Christ as it was to paint his betrothed, or the district nurse, or the grocer on the corner.

35. Umberto Boccioni
The City Rises, 1910
The Museum of Modern Art, New York

FUTURISM: A COUNTERCLAIM FROM ITALY

Apollinaire was, on the other hand, distinctly more wary of the young Italian painter who called on him in October, 1911. Umberto Boccioni was just 29 years old, and in three months' time he and his friends of the Italian Futurist group were to have an exhibition at Bernheim-Jeune, one of the foremost dealers' galleries in Paris; Apollinaire was known to have considerable influence, and Boccioni was there to soften him up.

It is unlikely that Apollinaire had ever seen a painting by Boccioni, but like many other people in Paris he had read the "Futurist Manifesto" when it was published on the first page of *Le Figaro* on February 20, 1909. This "foundation manifesto" was the work of the poet and publicist F. T. Marinetti, and it was addressed not specifically to painters and sculptors but to every

36. (*below left*) Umberto Boccioni
Dynamism of a Soccer Player, 1913
The Museum of Modern Art, New York

37. (*below*) Umberto Boccioni
The Noise of the Street Penetrates the House, 1911
Niedersächsische Landesgalerie, Hanover

Italian who believed in the possibility of what was later called "a third great Italy." Italy was being buried alive—so the argument ran—beneath the weight of its past. Between them the Roman Emperors and the Popes of the Renaissance were imposing a mandatory secondhandedness on every detail of Italian life. Only when the libraries had been burned down and the museums flooded out could Italians live in the here-and-now. Once delivered from their past, they would see what an unprecedented beauty was all around them. They would acknowledge, in other words, that a racing car with its "machinegun-like" action was more beautiful than that pride of the Louvre, the Winged Victory of Samothrace.

Marinetti was by all accounts persuasive enough when he got on his feet, and undeniably he was dealing with real problems in a potentially decisive way. It is not wholly his fault that his speeches in translation sound like Disneyland's idea of Walt Whitman; Italy in 1909 was stagnant enough, in cultural terms, for there to be a genuine novelty about his "We shall sing of great crowds in the excitement of labor, relaxation and rebellion; of the many colored and polyphonic wave-break of revolution in modern cities; of the vibration by night of arsenals and factories beneath their violent electric moons; of bridges leaping like gymnasts and barrel-chested locomotives prancing on the rails like gigantic steel horses." It was quite true that Italy had been for too long the preserve of professors and librarians and dealers in antiques. But there were disquieting overtones to the over-dressed little demagogue with his popping eyes, his two protruding inches of stiff white shirt-cuff, his upturned mustaches and his English-style derby hat askew on his head. We have seen enough of "violence, cruelty and injustice" since Marinetti was around to resent the enthusiasm with which he preached that they should be the only subject matter of art. We don't want to hear from him or from anyone else that "war is the only health-giving thing in the world," or that women are by definition despicable, or that the burning of books is one of the highest forms of patriotism.

But when all that is said, it remains true that Marinetti was acting in the best interests of Italy. Futurism, in the sense of an unmixed belief in the future, was still more promising than a backward glance misted over with awe. If we can speak of the Italian achievement in design since 1950 as something that has set new standards in every department of consumption, Marinetti and the Futurists are somewhere at the back of it. But for them, Fiat Motors might be copying the chariot in Piero della Francesca's *Triumph of the Duke and Duchess of Urbino,* and Olivetti might be prowling around the Vatican for a table to go

38. Carlo Carrà
Funeral of the Anarchist Galli, 1911
The Museum of Modern Art, New York

39. (*below*) Giacomo Balla
Swifts: Paths of Movement, Dynamic Sequences, 1913
The Museum of Modern Art, New York

40. Gino Severini
The Armored Train, 1915
Richard S. Zeisler, New York

with Marinetti. The painters concerned were Umberto Boccioni, Carlo Carrà, Giacomo Balla, Gino Severini and Luigi Russolo. Severini lived in Paris and knew what was going on there; he had seen, therefore, with what a delicate and continuous historical awareness French painting had been brought into the 20th century. He must have known also that it was one thing for his colleagues to stand up and talk their heads off on the stage of a theater in Turin, and quite another for them to come across with paintings that would hold their own in the context of what was being done in Paris. It was for this reason, and at Severini's suggestion, that Marinetti sent Boccioni and Carrà to Paris, at his own expense, in October, 1911.

Once again, Marinetti was quite right. It would not do at all for the Futurist painters to make fools of themselves in Paris; there was far too great a gap between their ambitions, as set out in March–April, 1910, and their performance. From our point of view, however, the interesting thing is not that they should have fallen short of their aims, but that those aims should have been so concisely and so cogently formulated. A great part of modern sensibility is foreshadowed in the "Technical Manifesto of Futurist Painting," to which Boccioni, Carrà, Balla, Severini and Russolo put their names in April, 1910. Before long there was a large international audience for what they had to say: notably for such pugnacious opinions as that "all forms of imitation are to be despised," that "all subjects previously used must be discarded," and that "what was truth for the painters of yesterday is falsehood for the painters of today." It was the power of these ideas, and not the degree of their fulfillment, which spread the name of Futurism all over Europe and made it a constructive force even after Marinetti himself had been discredited.

What Boccioni and his friends had to say was comparatively free from the militaristic verbiage with which Marinetti seasoned his public appearances. It had affinities of a more exalted sort: with Henri Bergson, for instance, whose *Matter and Memory* was first published in 1910. Bergson believed that there was something ridiculous in the idea—fundamental to most pre-Futurist painting—of an object stilled and isolated. Not only was the interpenetration of past and present one of the cornerstones of his philosophy, but he believed that an object owes its essence and existence to its environment and could not possibly exist by itself. A fixed object in a fixed space was an academic fiction, therefore. Boccioni and his friends were saying meanwhile that "space no longer exists. . . . Our bodies penetrate the sofas on which we sit, and those sofas penetrate our bodies. The motorbus rushes into the houses which it passes, and the houses in turn throw themselves on the motorbus and mingle with it." Insofar as pre-

with their smallest computer. It was thanks to Marinetti that the here-and-now got through in Italy and a rethought, radical and supremely intelligent approach to design was adopted not long after Mussolini (much admired by Marinetti, by the way) had brought the country near to ruin and been hung up by a meathook for his pains.

In the spring of 1910 five Italian painters made common cause

X. Gino Severini
Dynamic Hieroglyph of The Bal Tabarin, 1912
The Museum of Modern Art, New York

When Severini wrote his own "Futurist Manifesto" in 1913, he said among much else that "objects no longer exist." The notion of the integrality of matter had been utterly destroyed in the sciences, and it was time for it to be utterly destroyed in art also. To put this into practice Severini took that classic Parisian subject, the dance hall, and restated it in a new and complex picture language derived in part from his fellow Futurists, from odds and ends of Cubist practice (the use, for example, of words, whole or fragmented), from the color theories of Robert Delaunay, and from a flickering, all-over animation of the surface which did not exclude a certain amount of realistic anatomical detail. The method was a mess, dialectically speaking; but in this big painting it worked, thanks to the overriding physical energy of the conception and to a superabundance of gossipy detail.

41. Medardo Rosso
The Golden Age (or *Wife and Son*), 1886
Mr. and Mrs. Joseph Tanenbaum, Toronto

CURSE **3**
WITH EXPLETIVE OF WHIRLWIND
THE BRITANNIC ÆSTHETE
CREAM OF THE SNOBBISH EARTH
ROSE OF SHARON OF GOD-PRIG
OF SIMIAN VANITY
SNEAK AND SWOT OF THE SCHOOL-
ROOM
IMBERB (or Berbed when in Belsize)-**PEDANT**
PRACTICAL JOKER
DANDY
CURATE

BLAST all products of phlegmatic cold
Life of **LOOKER-ON.**
CURSE
SNOBBERY
(disease of femininity)
FEAR OF RIDICULE
(arch vice of inactive, sleepy)
PLAY
STYLISM
SINS AND PLAGUES
of this **LYMPHATIC** finished
(we admit in every sense
finished)
VEGETABLE HUMANITY.

42. Page from *Blast,* issue
No. 1, June, 1914
Edited by Wyndham Lewis
Published: London, John
Lane, The Bodley Head

Blast was a short-lived (two numbers only) periodical, edited in London by painter, novelist and controversialist Wyndham Lewis. Its contributors included T. S. Eliot, Ezra Pound and Lewis himself; and it specialized (as here) in the use of typography as an instrument of aggression. Lewis got the idea from the Italian Futurists, but it was ideally suited to his own combative nature and gift for polemic.

vious art had concerned itself with the "universal dynamism" which seemed to the Futurists the basic principle of life, it had focused on a notional fixed moment within it. Futurism aimed to set down on the canvas "the dynamic sensation itself, eternalized." Previous art had given a restricted and pedestrian account of man's potential; now that the full extent of that potential had been revealed by science, it was for art to catch up. The material nature of bodies had been revealed by science as no more than a convenient figure of speech; art should forthwith admit that, in the words of the Technical Manifesto, "movement and light destroy the materiality of bodies."

To all this there had seemed to be no natural Italian ancestor. At most the sculptor Medardo Rosso could be advanced as having once said that "in space, nothing is material." Rosso was reported in 1909 as having made mock of conventional sculpture,

in which "forms are shaved off from the whirling center of universal life, remaining there stiff and still to be gaped at by the inquisitive spectator." Far better, he said, that the intensity of feeling in a work should "impel it out into space, radiating out to infinity in the way that an electric wave flies out to rejoin the eternal force of the universe." Rosso was, therefore, on the Futurists' side; but Rosso lived in Paris and was in virtual retirement. The Futurists had said what they were going to do; now they had to go out and do it, on their own.

If Paris gave them a rough ride at the first exhibition of Futurist painting in February, 1912, it was partly because they attempted to prejudge their own exhibition by saying that it established them as "the leaders of the European movement in painting." In particular, they derided Cubism for its reliance on the idea of the motionless object. Now, it is perfectly true that Cubism is an

43. David Bomberg
Mud Bath, c. 1913–14
The Tate Gallery, London

The most distinctive of British contributions to the international avant-garde before 1914 was made by David Bomberg. The son of Polish immigrant parents, Bomberg lived in one of the poorest quarters of London; the picture reproduced here is set in Schevzik's Steam Baths, and, despite a mechanistic element in the portrayal of the figures, it deals with real people in a real situation: diving into the water; outlined against the red area of the bath itself; or taking their ease on its yellow surround. In spite of his disadvantaged position, Bomberg was in touch with all that was newest in Paris. Brancusi, Duchamp-Villon and Marinetti were among those who saw his first one-man exhibition in London in 1914.

art of equilibrium, and that in the hands of second-rate artists an art of equilibrium becomes an art of stasis. It was not only the Italian Futurists who were to complain in time of the restrictions of the Cubist grid. But in several of the paintings which he showed in Paris, Boccioni, for one, borrowed heavily from the Cubist paintings by Gleizes and Metzinger which he had seen in the Salon d'Automne a month or two before; this was not quite, therefore, the moment at which to make fun of them.

"Sheer idiocy" was how Apollinaire summed up the Futurists' pretensions; and there were others in Paris who said that if the Futurists wanted to burn down the Italian museums it was because they couldn't stand the competition. And of course many of the key works of Italian Futurism do still look both inept and graceless. But they don't look negligible, even so; somewhere within them there is an authenticity of effort which keeps them alive. And if Futurism in general never ceased to needle the Parisian—Apollinaire almost had to fight a duel in March, 1914, when Robert Delaunay and others thought he had become too much in its favor—it was because the Futurists were at grips with modernity in a way which could not quite be dismissed. Their paintings got on the mat with modern life in situations where the French had preferred to watch from the sidelines. Their paintings were awkward, but it was a necessary and honorable awkwardness. "It is an appalling burden," Boccioni wrote later, "to have to elaborate within oneself a whole lost century of painting."

Nor was it only to easel painting that Boccioni and his friends directed their attention. Russolo moved into music and by 1914 was anticipating the notion of John Cage that all noise is music if you know how to listen to it. Balla and Boccioni moved into sculpture, and by 1914–15 Balla had pioneered many ideas that

35

44. Umberto Boccioni
Unique Forms of Continuity in Space, 1913
The Museum of Modern Art, New York

were to be fundamental to later practice: that physical mass was not essential to sculptural form, for instance, and that sculpture could be transparent, highly colored, luminous and virtually incorporeal. Boccioni, above all, went on spawning ideas until he died in 1916 after falling from a horse. As had happened with his paintings, he issued his program first and then had to make the work to fit it. Already in April, 1912, he was writing that the figure in sculpture should be broken open in such a way that its environment became a part of it; that the "wonderful mathematical and geometrical elements" which science had lately put before us should be brought into sculpture and "embedded in the muscular lines of the body"; and that a sculpture need not be in one material only but could incorporate whatever could contribute most vividly to its emotional impact—"glass, wood, cardboard, iron, cement, horsehair, leather, cloth, mirrors, electric light, etc."

It is one of the ironies of art history that the finest of Boccioni's few surviving sculptures should remind us not so much of that stirring passage as of the masterpiece of antiquity which Marinetti had outlawed in 1909: the Winged Victory of Samothrace. *Unique Forms of Continuity in Space* (fig. 44) can, in fact, be read as much in terms of windblown draperies as of the lines of force which Boccioni had had in mind. But, once again, Boccioni's monument consists not so much in the surviving works as in the climate of total liberty which he promoted. Insofar as that total liberty is an integral part of the modern sensibility, Futurism initiated it. Its influence in that regard is still very far from exhausted: the notion of a disposable art—one that can be chalked on the floor or sent by telegram—has its origins in Marinetti. And if one day we settle for the state of affairs, long envisaged by R. Buckminster Fuller, in which buildings can be erected just for one season and thrown away at the end of it like paper handkerchiefs, that too will be the consummation of a Futurist attitude. ("It will be for each generation," the writ ran in 1911, "to build its own city.")

Apollinaire was sufficiently in tune with the times to know that Futurism had something real to offer. But he didn't care for the portentous tone, or for the seething inner hatred, or for the delight in physical assault; and although he responded to anything that stressed the newness and the idiosyncrasy of modern life, he was really much happier with the unquestioning and beatific attitude of Roger de La Fresnaye in his *The Conquest of the Air* (pl. I), or of Robert Delaunay in his *Homage to Blériot* (pl. XI). Quite apart from that, he responded best on a basis of personal contact; and during the period immediately before 1914 he was introduced to a completely new set of attitudes to art by his friendship with Marcel Duchamp and Francis Picabia.

XI. Robert Delaunay
Homage to Blériot, 1914
Kunstmuseum, Basel

45. Francis Picabia
Dances at the Spring, 1912
Philadelphia Museum of Art

47. Jacob Epstein
The Rock Drill, 1913–14
  (cast 1962)
The Museum of Modern
  Art, New York

The American-born sculptor Jacob Epstein was, for most of his long career, a famous and controversial figure in British art life. "It was in the experimental pre-war days of 1913," he once wrote, "that I was fired to do the Rock Drill. My ardour for machinery (short-lived) expended itself in the purchase of an actual drill, second-hand, and upon this I made and mounted a machine-like robot, visored, menacing and carrying within itself its progeny, protectively ensconced. Here is the armed sinister figure of today and tomorrow. . . . Later I lost my interest in machinery and discarded the drill. I cast in metal only the upper part of the figure." Despite its simplistic approach to the problem of man and his machines, *The Rock Drill* remains one of the most arresting images of its date.

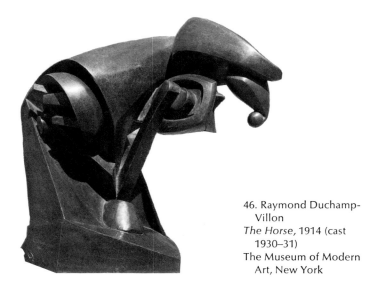

46. Raymond Duchamp-
  Villon
The Horse, 1914 (cast
  1930–31)
The Museum of Modern
  Art, New York

Raymond Duchamp-Villon was the second of three brothers, all of whom left their mark on the art of this century. (The eldest was the painter and engraver Jacques Villon; the youngest was Marcel Duchamp.) Duchamp-Villon had been a partisan of the age of steel since 1889, when he was taken to an industrial exhibition at the age of thirteen. In *The Horse* he took a subject from a pre-industrial phase of civilization and combined it with the "superior dynamism" which he believed to be characteristic of the machine age. The horse is unmistakably a horse, and yet it bears out what Duchamp-Villon once wrote: "The power of the machine imposes itself upon us to such an extent that we can scarcely imagine living bodies without it."

48. Francis Picabia
Portrait of Mistinguett, 1907
The Solomon R. Guggenheim Museum, New York

Mistinguett was one of the great French music hall performers of this century. When Picabia painted her he had yet to establish himself as a leader of the avant-garde, and was still working in a style derived from the flat color areas and bold linear drawing which had come into French painting by way of Gauguin, Fauve painting and the Japanese print.

THE BEGINNINGS OF DUCHAMP

It was by no means clear at that time that Marcel Duchamp was one of the most remarkable men of the 20th century and that Francis Picabia would turn out to have so many new ideas that he could never be bothered to follow any of them up very far. Duchamp in January, 1911, was simply the youngest and quite

49. Marcel Duchamp
The Artist's Father, 1910
Philadelphia Museum of Art

possibly the least gifted of the three sons of a provincial lawyer who were making a name for themselves in Paris as artists, certainly, but also as talkers and negotiators and spreaders of ideas. The oldest brother had taken the working name of Jacques Villon and was doing his best to graft a systematic and mathematical turn of mind onto the basically intuitive and pragmatical character of Cubism as it was practiced by Picasso and Braque. The second brother, Raymond Duchamp-Villon, was known to be tacking this way and that in the general direction of Cubist sculpture. As for Marcel Duchamp, he was 23 when he painted the relatively conservative portrait of his father (fig. 49), 24 when he

50. Marcel Duchamp
Portrait of Chess Players, 1911
Philadelphia Museum of Art

painted the *Portrait of Chess Players* (fig. 50) and still not yet 25 when he painted one of the most famous pictures of this century, the *Nude Descending a Staircase, No. 2* (pl. XII). He was, in other words, outstandingly precocious in an age when, more and more, the big men tended to mature slowly. When the Armory Show opened in New York on February 19, 1913, it was Duchamp, at 26, who touched the nerve of popular interest with the *Nude Descending a Staircase*, even though there were masterpieces on hand by men 10 and 20 years older than he.

Popular interest often goes astray, but in this case New Yorkers were more discerning than those of Duchamp's colleagues who railed against the *Nude Descending a Staircase* when he thought of showing it in the Salon des Indépendants in Paris in 1912. Duchamp's fellow Frenchmen regarded it as not authentically Cubist

XII. Marcel Duchamp
Nude Descending a Staircase, No. 2, 1912
Philadelphia Museum of Art

51. Giacomo Balla
Car in a Race, 1914
Art Gallery of Ontario,
Toronto

(in which they were quite right) and as a sell-out to Italian Futurism (in which they were quite wrong, in that the picture was completed by January, 1912, and at a time when no examples of Italian Futurist painting had been seen in Paris). Duchamp had been close enough to the auxiliary Cubists for them to read the picture as in some way a defection from their beliefs; and the issues raised by the Futurists were hot enough, in February and March, 1912, for certain people to lose their heads when presented with what was a demonstration of, among much else, the Futurist thesis that "on account of the persistence of an image upon the retina, moving objects constantly multiply and become deformed as they succeed one another like vibrations hurled into the space which they traverse." Notations of that are fundamen-

tal to such classics of Futurism as Balla's *Dog on a Leash* (fig. 53) and *Girl Running Along a Balcony* (fig. 52).

But both these pictures by Balla were painted after the *Nude Descending a Staircase*. Duchamp got the point all by himself, just as he got the point of chronophotography (the recording of human beings or animals in motion by means of successive photographic exposures) in the form in which it first came to notice late in the 19th century. Indeed, he brought about a coherent if temporary alliance between these ideas and the practice of Analytical Cubism; and this he did in that spirit of detached and mischievous inquiry which was to characterize so much of his later work. Duchamp was one of the quickest learners in the history of art, but what he had learned was never presented in an

52. Giacomo Balla
Girl Running Along a Balcony, 1912
Civica Galleria d'Arte Moderna, Milan

53. Giacomo Balla
Dog on a Leash, 1912
Buffalo Fine Arts Academy, N.Y.

unaltered, frontal way. It was angled: aligned, in other words, to certain steadfast preoccupations of his own.

The fascination of the *Nude Descending* does not derive from the successful crossbreeding of two idioms which were then much in the air. It has a more complex origin. Duchamp had been drawing and painting the female nude in one way or another since the beginning of 1910 (and in defiance, by the way, of the Futurists' ten-year veto on the painting of the nude). Few men have been more sensitive than he to the beauty of women, or more adroit in their acts of homage to it; but Duchamp was also very much aware both of the elements of comedy and indignity which beset all sexual relationships and of the absurdities inherent in the apparatus which Nature has provided for their fulfillment. Comparisons in this context with machinery, real or imagined, are sometimes to our advantage, sometimes not; either way, the subject in 1912 was wide open for further treatment.

Duchamp never liked to "explain" his work, in an everyday sense; but he never deliberately concealed its meanings, either, and when he said that he owed a great deal to Odilon Redon he meant, I think, that like Redon he enjoyed secreting one mystery within another. When Redon made his illustrations for Flaubert and for Edgar Allan Poe, he never produced a one-to-one realiza-

tion of ideas already explicit in the text. Duchamp, in the two versions of the *Nude Descending,* was starting from an idea suggested to him in a poem by Jules Laforgue; and the inner subject of the two paintings may well be the notion that even an ideal re-creation of feminine beauty, a machine freed from the imperfections of our real-life anatomy, would nonetheless end up looking much like the clanking, ungainly and fallible bag of bones that is already familiar to us. No fulfilled work of art has any one definitive explanation; but it is because this idea is one of many that can be put forward and not quite laughed out of existence that the *Nude Descending* still bears endless discussion.

The Armory Show was not the last manifestation of the pacific International. Nor was it even the grandest thing of its sort; that title should go to the Autumn Salon of 1913 in Berlin, where virtually everything that has been discussed here was represented in an ideally ample way, together with the debuts of Americans like Marsden Hartley and Germans like Max Ernst. But the Armory Show has a special significance for us here, in that thereafter America was wide open to the new; and with the arrival in New York of Francis Picabia in 1913, and of Marcel Duchamp in 1915, there occurred a significant shift in the geography of modern art.

SUGGESTED READINGS

Futurism

Dorazio, Virginia D. *Giacomo Balla: An Album of His Life and Work.*
    New York, Wittenborn, 1969.

Kirby, Michael. *Futurist Performance.*
    New York, Dutton, 1971.

Marinetti, Filippo Tommaso. *Selected Writings.* R. W. Flint, ed.
    New York, Farrar, Straus and Giroux, 1971.

Martin, Marianne W. *Futurist Art and Theory, 1909–1915.*
    New York, Oxford University Press, 1968.

Taylor, Joshua C. *Futurism.*
    New York, The Museum of Modern Art, 1961.

Toffler, Alvin, ed. *The Futurists.*
    New York, Random House, 1972.

Guillaume Apollinaire

Breunig, Leroy C., ed. *Apollinaire on Art: Essays and Reviews, 1902–1918.*
    (Documents of 20th-Century Art ser.)
    New York, Viking, 1972.

Shattuck, Roger. *The Banquet Years: The Origins of the Avant-Garde in France,
1885 to World War I.* Rev. ed.
    New York, Vintage Books, 1968.

Marc Chagall

Cassou, Jean. *Chagall.* (World of Art ser.)
    New York, Praeger, 1965.

Crespelle, Jean-Paul. *Chagall.*
    New York, Coward-McCann, 1970.

Lassaigne, Jacques. *Chagall: Drawings and Watercolors for the Ballet.*
    (Art Reference Library ser.)
    New York, Tudor, 1969.

Meyer, Franz. *Marc Chagall.*
    New York, Abrams, 1963.

Robert and Sonia Delaunay

Damase, Jacques, Delaunay, Sonia, and others. *Sonia Delaunay: Rhythms
and Colors.*
    Greenwich, Conn., New York Graphic Society, 1972.

Vriesen, Gustav, and Imdahl, Max. *Robert Delaunay: Light and Color.*
    New York, Abrams, 1969.

Marcel Duchamp

Cabanne, Pierre. *Dialogues with Marcel Duchamp.* (Documents of
20th-Century Art ser.)
    New York, Viking, 1971.

d'Harnoncourt, Anne, and McShine, Kynaston, eds. *Marcel Duchamp.*
    New York, The Museum of Modern Art, 1973.

Lebel, Robert. *Marcel Duchamp.*
    New York, Grossman, 1967.

Paz, Octavio. *Marcel Duchamp or The Castle of Purity.*
    London, Cape Goliard Press in association with New York, Grossman, 1970.

Schwarz, Arturo. *The Complete Works of Marcel Duchamp.*
    New York, Abrams, 1969.

Wassily Kandinsky

Grohmann, Will. *Wassily Kandinsky: Life and Work.*
    New York, Abrams, 1958.

Kandinsky, Wassily. *Concerning the Spiritual in Art and Painting in Particular,
1912.* (Documents of Modern Art reprint ser.)
    New York, Wittenborn, 1970.

Kandinsky, Wassily, and Marc, Franz. *The Blaue Reiter Almanac.*
    (Documents of 20th-Century Art ser.)
    New York, Viking, 1972.

Overy, Paul. *Kandinsky: The Language of the Eye.*
    New York, Praeger, 1969.

Franz Marc

Lankheit, Klaus. *Franz Marc: Watercolors, Drawings, Writings.*
    New York, Abrams, 1960.

Henri Rousseau

Rich, Daniel Catton. *Henri Rousseau.* Reprint.
    First publ. 1942. New York, Arno for The Museum of Modern Art, 1970.

Vallier, Dora. *Henri Rousseau.*
    New York, Abrams, 1964

LIST OF ILLUSTRATIONS

Dimensions: height precedes width; a third dimension, depth, is given for sculptures and constructions where relevant. Foreign titles are in English, except in cases where the title does not translate or is better known in its original form. Asterisked titles indicate works reproduced in color.

Balla, Giacomo
(1871–1958)

Girl Running Along a Balcony, 1912 (fig. 52)
Oil on canvas, 50 x 50 inches
Civica Galleria d'Arte Moderna, Milan

Dog on a Leash, 1912 (fig. 53)
Oil on canvas, 35⅜ x 43¼ inches
Courtesy George F. Goodyear and the
Buffalo Fine Arts Academy, N.Y.

Swifts: Paths of Movement, Dynamic Sequences,
1913 (fig. 39)
Oil on canvas, 38⅛ x 47¼ inches
The Museum of Modern Art, New York
Purchase

Car in a Race, 1914 (fig. 51)
Brush, tempera and ink on paper mounted on
canvas, 21¼ x 28⅞ inches
Art Gallery of Ontario, Toronto
Gift of Sam and Ayala Zacks, 1970

Page from *Blast*, issue No. 1, June, 1914 (fig. 42)
Edited by Wyndham Lewis. Published:
London, John Lane, The Bodley Head

Boccioni, Umberto
(1882–1916)

The City Rises, 1910 (fig. 35)
Oil on canvas, 6 feet 6½ inches x 9 feet 10½
inches
The Museum of Modern Art, New York
Mrs. Simon Guggenheim Fund

The Noise of the Street Penetrates the House,
1911 (fig. 37)
Oil on canvas, 40 x 40½ inches
Niedersächsische Landesgalerie, Hanover

Dynamism of a Soccer Player, 1913 (fig. 36)
Oil on canvas, 6 feet 4⅛ inches x 6 feet 7⅛
inches
The Museum of Modern Art, New York
The Sidney and Harriet Janis Collection

Unique Forms of Continuity in Space, 1913
(fig. 44)
Bronze, 43⅞ x 34⅞ x 15¾ inches
The Museum of Modern Art, New York
Acquired through the Lillie P. Bliss Bequest

Bomberg, David
(1890–1957)

Mud Bath, c. 1913–14 (fig. 43)
Oil on canvas, 60 x 88¼ inches
The Tate Gallery, London

Carrà, Carlo
(1881–1966)

Funeral of the Anarchist Galli, 1911 (fig. 38)
Oil on canvas, 6 feet 6¼ inches x 8 feet 6 inches
The Museum of Modern Art, New York
Acquired through the Lillie P. Bliss Bequest

Chagall, Marc
(b. 1887)

Half Past Three (The Poet), 1911 (fig. 32)
Oil on canvas, 77½ x 57½ inches
Philadelphia Museum of Art
The Louise and Walter Arensberg Collection

Birth, 1911 (fig. 29)
Oil on canvas, 44¼ x 76⅛ inches
The Art Institute of Chicago
Gift of Mr. and Mrs. Maurice E. Culberg

Homage to Apollinaire, 1911–12 (fig. 33)
Oil on canvas, 82 x 78 inches
Stedelijk van Abbe Museum, Eindhoven

Calvary, 1912 (pl. IX)
Oil on canvas, 68¾ x 75¾ inches
The Museum of Modern Art, New York
Acquired through the Lillie P. Bliss Bequest

Self-Portrait with Seven Fingers, 1912 (fig. 30)
Oil on canvas, 50⅜ x 42⅛ inches
Stedelijk Museum, Amsterdam

Burning House, 1913 (fig. 31)
Oil on canvas, 41⅞ x 47¼ inches
The Solomon R. Guggenheim Museum, New York

Over Vitebsk (after a painting of 1914), 1915–20
(fig. 34)
Oil on canvas, 26⅜ x 36½ inches
The Museum of Modern Art, New York
Acquired through the Lillie P. Bliss Bequest

Delaunay, Robert
(1885–1941)

Eiffel Tower, 1910 (fig. 14)
Oil on canvas, 79¾ x 54⅝ inches
The Solomon R. Guggenheim Museum, New York

The Cardiff Team, 1912–13 (fig. 11)
Oil on canvas, 78¼ x 52 inches
Stedelijk van Abbe Museum, Eindhoven

Sun Disks, 1912–13 (fig. 12)
Oil on canvas, diameter 53 inches
The Museum of Modern Art, New York
Mrs. Simon Guggenheim Fund

Sun, Tower and Airplane, 1913 (fig. 13)
Oil on canvas, 52 x 51⅛ inches
Albright-Knox Art Gallery, Buffalo, N.Y.

Homage to Blériot, 1914 (pl. XI)
Distemper on canvas, 8 feet 4 inches x 8 feet 4½
inches
Kunstmuseum, Basel

Delaunay, Sonia
(b. 1885)

The Bal Bullier, 1913 (pl. III)
Oil on canvas, 38¾ inches x 13 feet
Musée National d'Art Moderne, Paris

Duchamp, Marcel
(1887–1968)

The Artist's Father, 1910 (fig. 49)
Oil on canvas, 36⅜ x 28⅞ inches
Philadelphia Museum of Art
The Louise and Walter Arensberg Collection

Portrait of Chess Players, 1911 (fig. 50)
Oil on canvas, 39¾ x 39¾ inches
Philadelphia Museum of Art
The Louise and Walter Arensberg Collection

Nude Descending a Staircase, No. 2, 1912 (pl. XII)
Oil on canvas, 58 x 35 inches
Philadelphia Museum of Art
The Louise and Walter Arensberg Collection

Duchamp-Villon, Raymond
(1876–1918)

The Horse, 1914 (fig. 46)
Bronze (cast 1930–31), 40 x 39½ x 22⅜ inches
The Museum of Modern Art, New York
Van Gogh Purchase Fund

Epstein, Jacob
(1880–1959)

The Rock Drill, 1913–14 (fig. 47)
Bronze (cast 1962), 28 x 26 inches
The Museum of Modern Art, New York
Mrs. Simon Guggenheim Fund

Gauguin, Paul
(1848–1903)

Loss of Virginity, 1890–91 (fig. 7)
Oil on canvas, 34 x 50 inches
Chrysler Museum at Norfolk, Virginia
Gift of Walter P. Chrysler, Jr.

Gleizes, Albert
(1881–1953)

Harvest Threshing, 1912 (fig. 6)
Oil on canvas, 8 feet 10 inches x 11 feet 6 inches
The Solomon R. Guggenheim Museum, New York

Gontcharova, Nathalie
(1881–1962)

"Le Coq d'Or" (Scenery design for
        Diaghilev's Ballets Russes, Paris, 1914; fig. 28)
Gouache on cardboard, 18⅜ x 24¼ inches
The Museum of Modern Art, New York
Acquired through the Lillie P. Bliss Bequest

Jawlensky, Alexej von
(1864–1941)

Landscape, Murnau, 1910 (fig. 19)
Oil on cardboard, 20 x 21 inches
Kunstmuseum, Düsseldorf

Cover design for *Jugend,* August 14, 1897,
        by H. Christiansen (fig. 15)
11¼ x 8¾ inches
Published: Munich and Leipzig, G. Hirth

Kandinsky, Wassily
(1866–1944)

Phalanx: First Exhibition, 1901 (fig. 16)
Lithograph, 19½ x 26½ inches
The Museum of Modern Art, New York
Gift of Mme. Wassily Kandinsky

Russian Beauty in a Landscape, 1905 (fig. 17)
Tempera on black paper, 16½ x 11¼ inches
Städtische Galerie im Lenbachhaus, Munich

Study for "Landscape with a Tower," 1908 (fig. 22)
Oil on board, 13 x 17⅝ inches
The Solomon R. Guggenheim Museum, New York

*Mountain, 1909 (pl. VI)
Oil on cardboard, 43¼ x 43¼ inches
Städtische Galerie im Lenbachhaus, Munich

* *Landscape near Murnau,* 1909 (pl. IV)
Oil on board, 19⅞ x 25⅝ inches
The Solomon R. Guggenheim Museum, New York

* *Composition No. 2,* 1910 (pl. V)
Oil on canvas, 38⅜ x 51¾ inches
The Solomon R. Guggenheim Museum, New York

Winter Study with Church, 1911 (fig. 25)
Oil on board, 13 x 17⅝ inches
The Solomon R. Guggenheim Museum, New York

Pastorale, No. 132, 1911 (fig. 23)
Oil on canvas, 41⅞ x 61¾ inches
The Solomon R. Guggenheim Museum, New York

Improvisation No. 30, 1913 (fig. 24)
Oil on canvas, 43¼ x 43¾ inches
The Art Institute of Chicago
Arthur Jerome Eddy Memorial Collection

Panel (3), 1914 (fig. 20)
Oil on canvas, 64 x 36¼ inches
Panel (4), 1914 (fig. 21)
Oil on canvas, 64 x 31½ inches
The Museum of Modern Art, New York
Mrs. Simon Guggenheim Fund

La Fresnaye, Roger de
(1885–1925)

**The Conquest of the Air,* 1913 (pl. I)
Oil on canvas, 92⅞ x 77 inches
The Museum of Modern Art, New York
Mrs. Simon Guggenheim Fund

Larionov, Mikhail
(1881–1964)

**Soldier on a Horse,* c. 1908–11 (pl. VIII)
Oil on canvas, 34¼ x 39 inches
The Tate Gallery, London

Laurencin, Marie
(1885–1956)

Group of Artists, 1908 (fig. 5)
Oil on canvas, 24¾ x 31⅛ inches
The Baltimore Museum of Art
The Cone Collection

Léger, Fernand
(1881–1955)

The Wedding, 1910–11 (fig. 1)
Oil on canvas, 8 feet 5 inches x 6 feet 9 inches
Musée National d'Art Moderne, Paris

Woman in Blue, 1912 (fig. 2)
Oil on canvas, 77 x 52 inches
Öffentliche Kunstsammlung, Basel

Macke, August
(1887–1914)

Making Fun of The Blue Rider, 1913 (fig. 26)
Watercolor, 9¾ x 13¾ inches
Städtische Galerie im Lenbachhaus, Munich

Marc, Franz
(1880–1916)

*Half-length Portrait of Henri Rousseau
        with Long Mustache,* 1911 (fig. 9)
Painting on glass, 6 x 4¼ inches
Städtische Galerie im Lenbachhaus, Munich

**The Blue Horse I,* 1911 (pl. VII)
Oil on canvas, 44¾ x 33¾ inches
Städtische Galerie im Lenbachhaus, Munich

The Unfortunate Land of Tyrol, 1913 (fig. 27)
Oil on canvas, 52 x 79 inches
The Solomon R. Guggenheim Museum, New York

Marcoussis, Louis
(1883–1941)

Portrait of Guillaume Apollinaire, 1912–20 (fig. 4)
Etching and drypoint, 19½ x 11 inches
The Museum of Modern Art, New York
Given anonymously

Münter, Gabriele
(1877–1962)

Man at a Table, 1911 (fig. 18)
Oil on cardboard, 20½ x 27 inches
Städtische Galerie, Munich

Picabia, Francis
(1879–1953)

Portrait of Mistinguett, 1907 (fig. 48)
Oil on canvas, 24 x 19¾ inches
The Solomon R. Guggenheim Museum, New York

Dances at the Spring, 1912 (fig. 45)
Oil on canvas, 47½ x 47½ inches
Philadelphia Museum of Art
The Louise and Walter Arensberg Collection

Picasso, Pablo
(1881–1973)

Portrait of Apollinaire, 1905 (fig. 3)
Ink and wash, 12½ x 9¼ inches
Private collection, Washington, D.C.

Rosso, Medardo
(1858–1928)

The Golden Age (or *Wife and Son*), 1886 (fig. 41)
Wax over plaster, 19 inches high
Mr. and Mrs. Joseph Tanenbaum, Toronto

Rousseau, Henri
(1844–1910)

The Sleeping Gypsy, 1897 (fig. 8)
Oil on canvas, 51 x 79 inches
The Museum of Modern Art, New York
Gift of Mrs. Simon Guggenheim

The Poet and His Muse, 1909 (fig. 10)
Oil on canvas, 58¼ x 38½ inches
Kunstmuseum, Basel

The Dream, 1910 (pl. II)
Oil on canvas, 6 feet 8½ inches x 9 feet 9½ inches
The Museum of Modern Art, New York
Gift of Nelson A. Rockefeller

Severini, Gino
(1883–1966)

Dynamic Hieroglyph of The Bal Tabarin, 1912
    (pl. X)
Oil on canvas with sequins, 63⅝ x 61½ inches
The Museum of Modern Art, New York
Acquired through the Lillie P. Bliss Bequest

The Armored Train, 1915 (fig. 40)
Oil on canvas, 46 x 34½ inches
Richard S. Zeisler, New York

PHOTOGRAPH CREDITS